SCHIRMER'S LIBRARY
OF MUSICAL CLASSICS

Vol. 2098

FRANZ WOHLFAHRT

Collected Easy Studies
For the Violin
Op. 45, 54, and 74

ISBN 978-1-4768-7727-3

G. SCHIRMER, Inc.

DISTRIBUTED BY

7777 W. BLUEMOUND RD. P.O. BOX 13819 MILWAUKEE, WI 53213

www.musicsalesclassical.com
www.halleonard.com

CONTENTS

Fifty Easy Melodius Studies,
Op. 74, Book I

Fifty Easy Melodius Studies,
Op. 74, Book II

Sixty Studies
Op. 45, Book I

Franz Wohlfahrt
(1833–1884)

Hold the fingers down as long as possible.
The left wrist very quiet.

In the second, third and seventh Études the same bowings
that were given for the first Etude are to be used.

Allegretto

4.

Moderato

5.

Pay attention to G♯ on the D-string and to D on the A-string.
Look out for D on the A-string and for A♭ on the E-string.

Allegro

15.

14

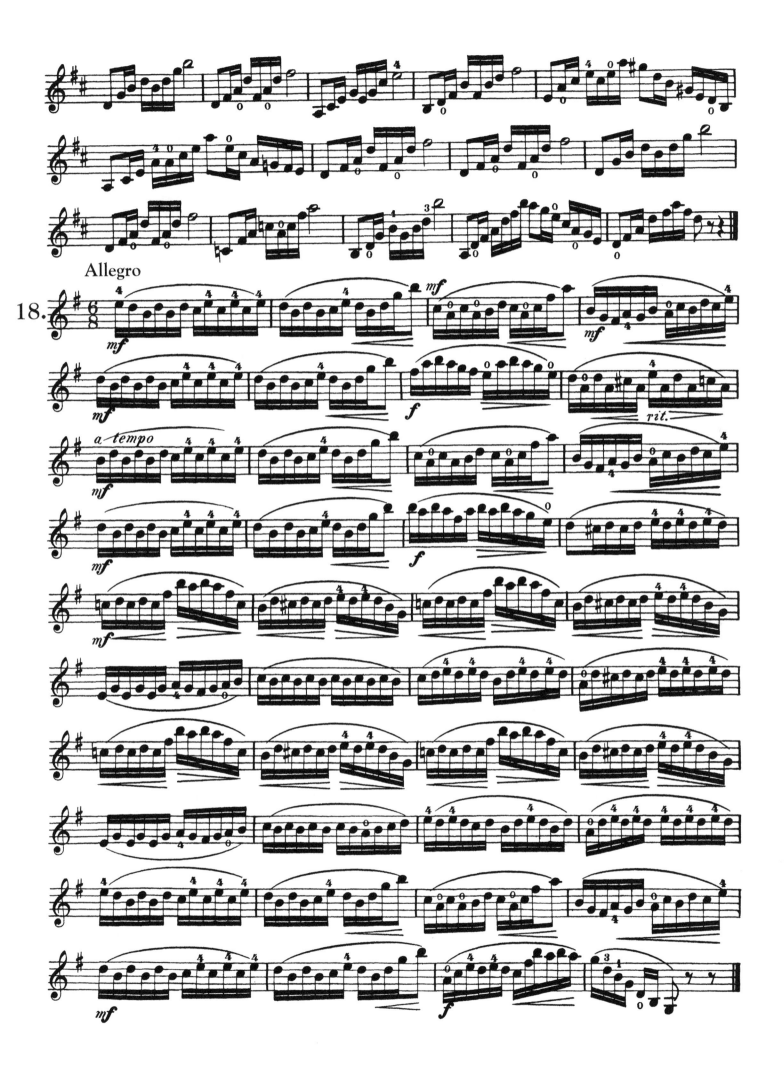

In the last three measures, employ the same bowing without change.

Allegro moderato

19.

Allegro

20.

Allegro

21.

Allegro

22.

Moderato

23.

29.

Moderato

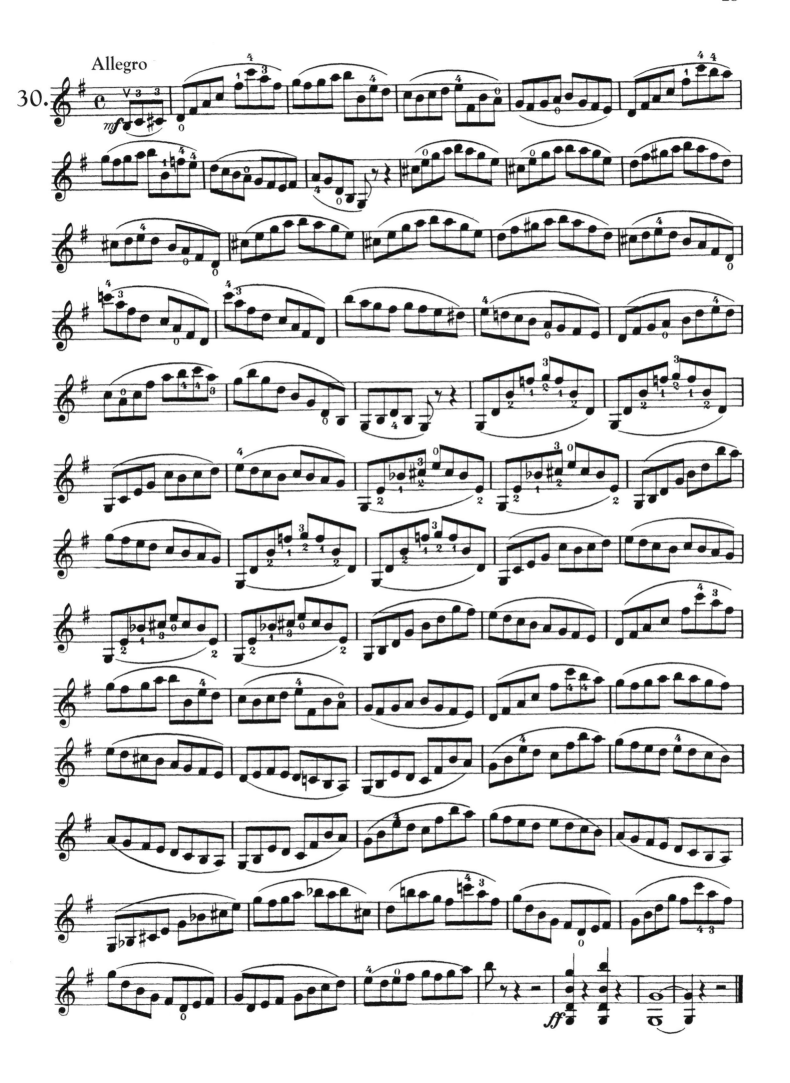

Sixty Studies
Op. 45, Book II

Franz Wohlfahrt
(1833–1884)

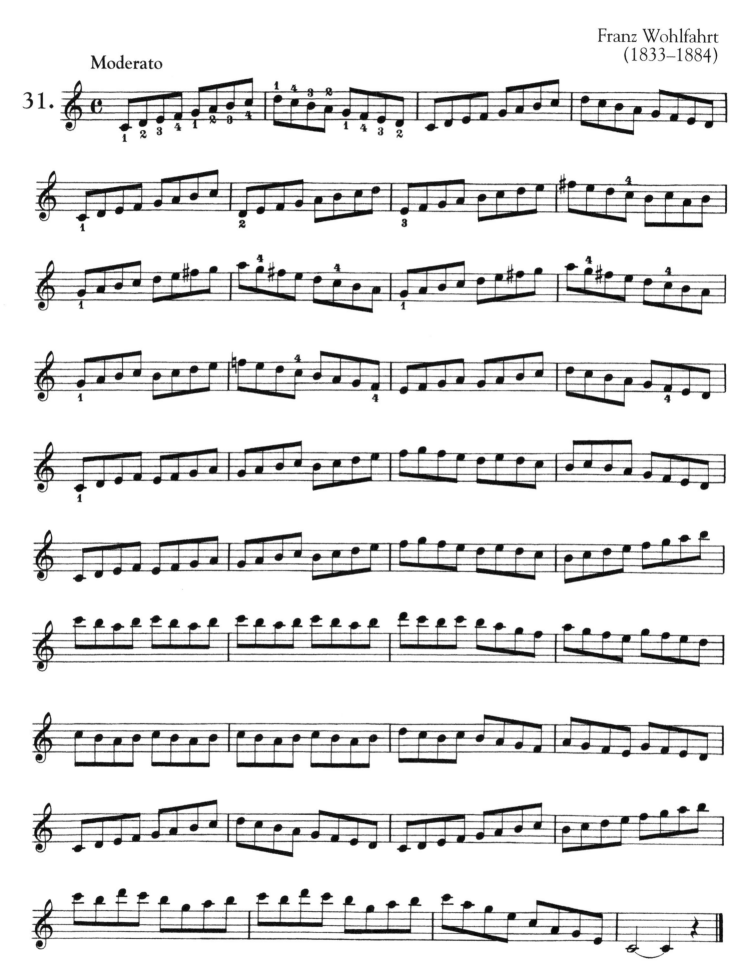

Allegro

32.

Allegro moderato

Allegro

34.

Allegro

35.

Moderato

38.

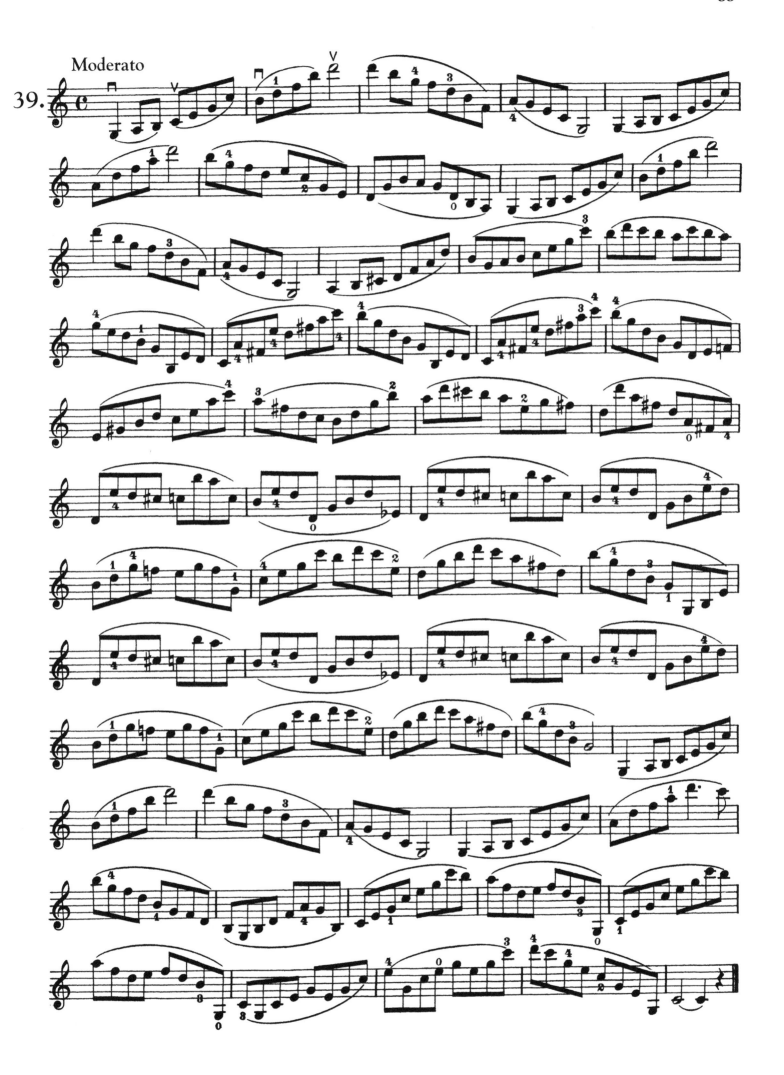

Allegro scherzando

Springing bow (ricochet)

40.

Allegro moderato

41.

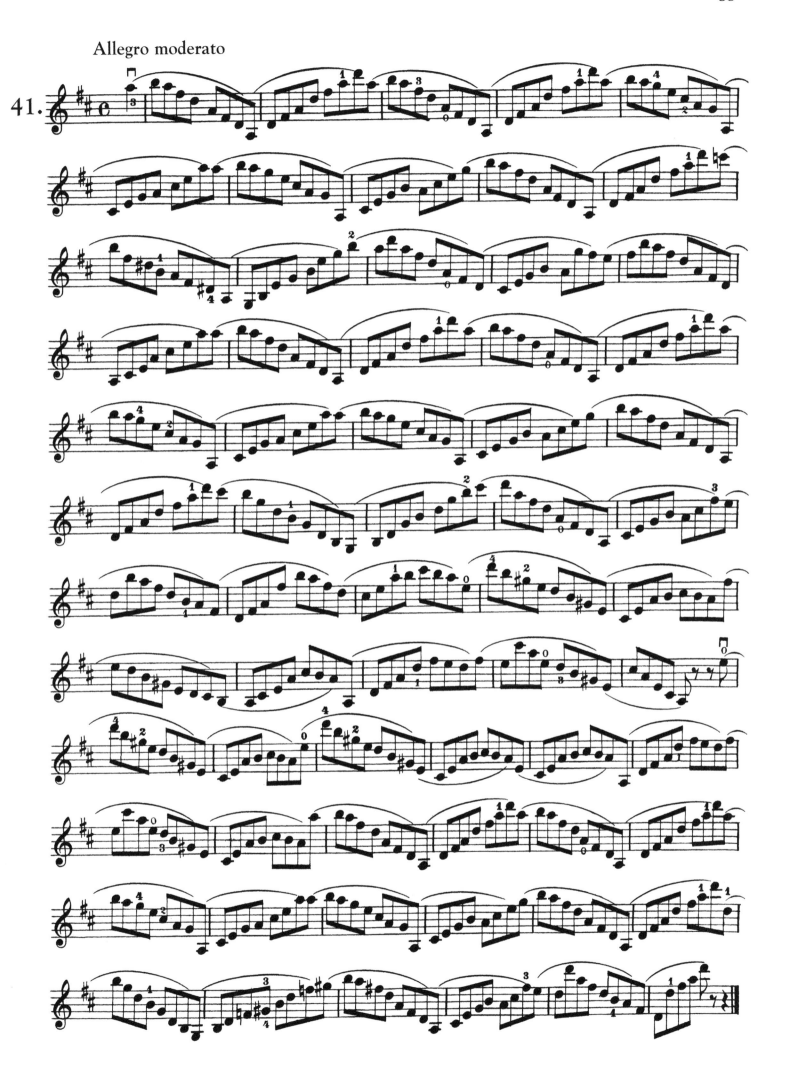

Andante

42.

Moderato

43.

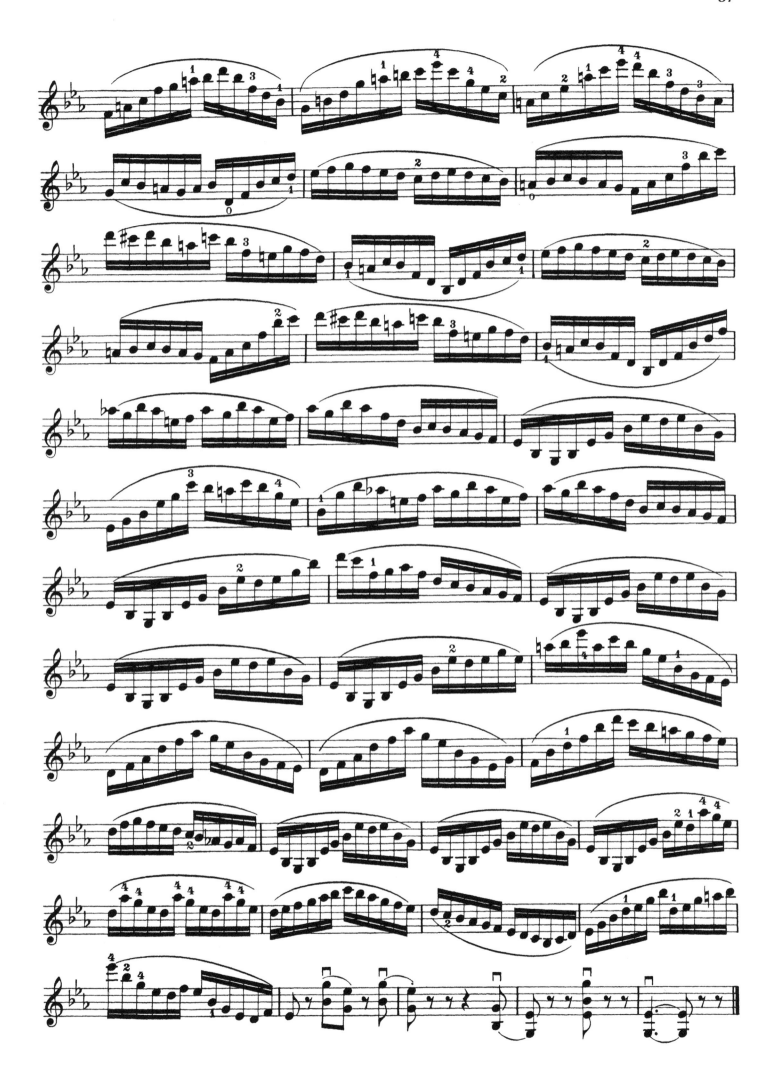

Tempo di marcia

44.

Moderato

45.

Andante cantabile

47.

42

Allegro

50.

Moderato

51.

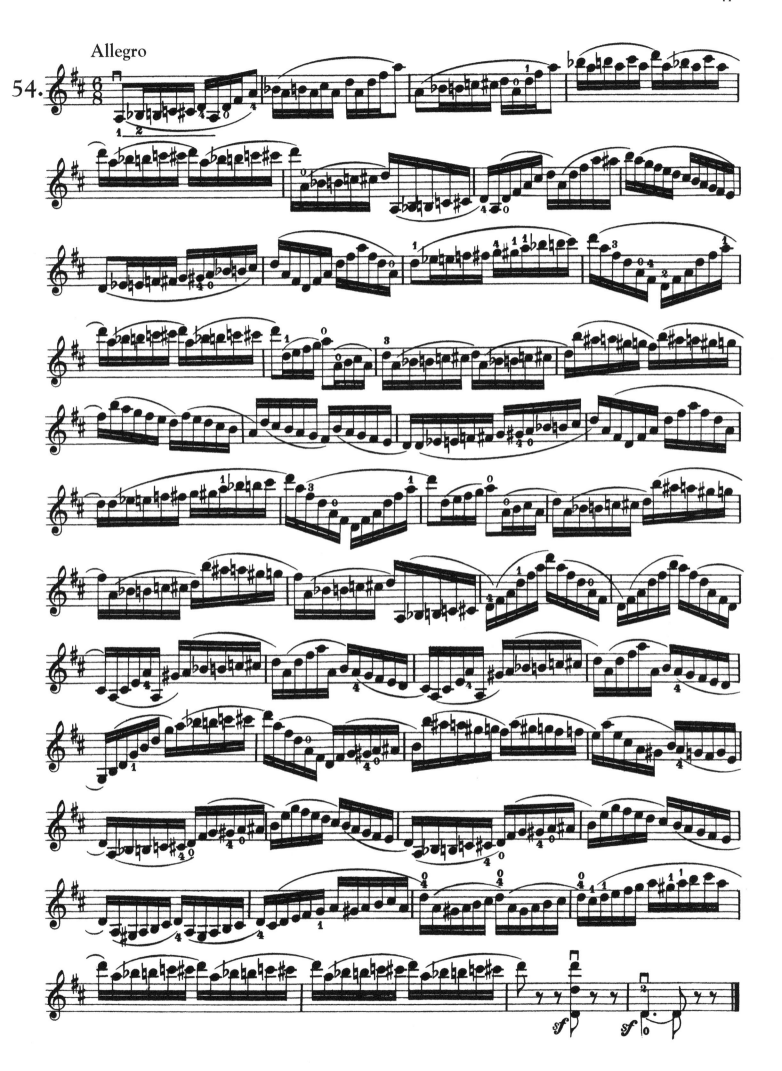

48

Allegro

55.

Moderato assai

57.

Andante

58.

Allegro con fuoco

60.

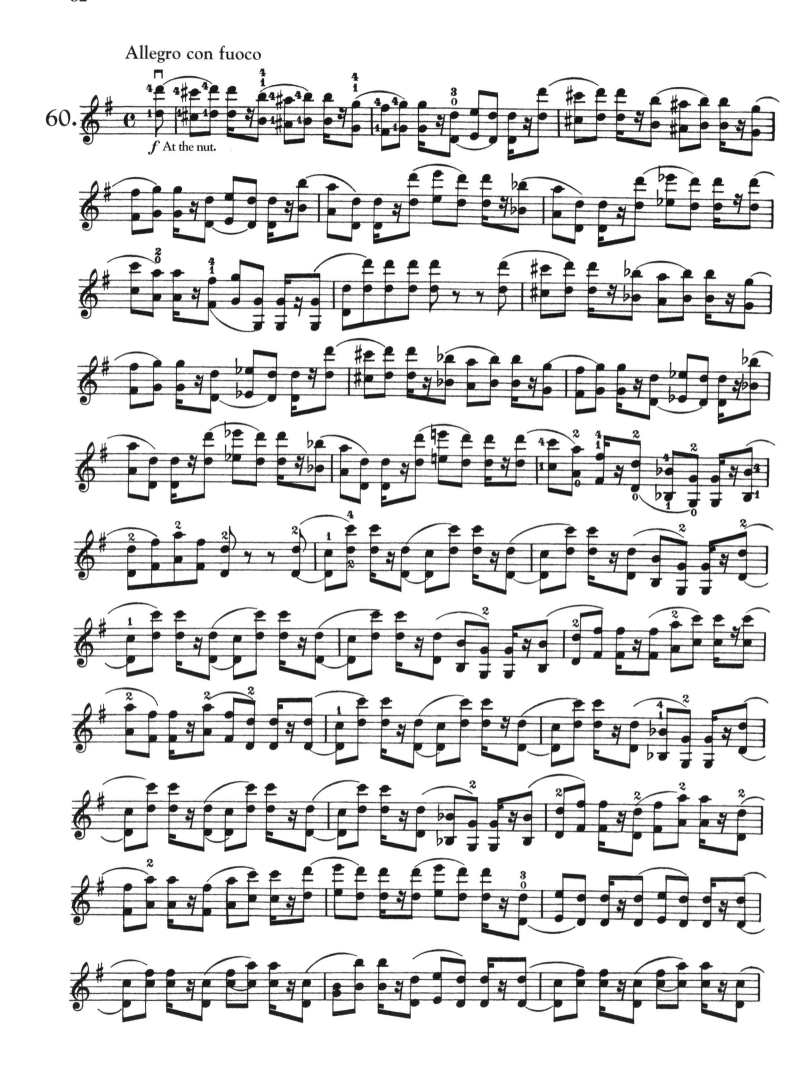

f At the nut.

Forty Elementary Etudes
Op. 54

Franz Wohlfahrt
(1833–1884)

Moderato Different bowings are to be employed in practising this Study

23.

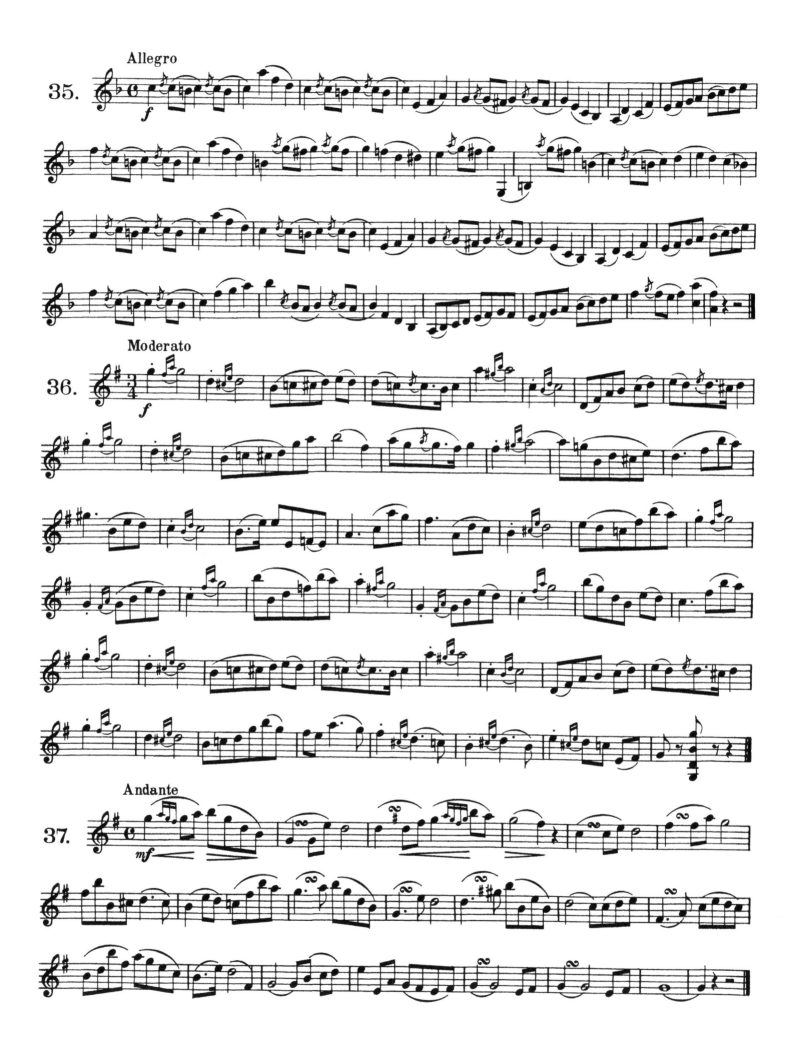

LABORUM
DULCE
LENIMEN

G. SCHIRMER

Fifty Easy Melodious Studies
Op. 74, Book I

Franz Wohlfahrt
(1833–1884)

Allegro moderato

2.

Allegro moderato

3.

Allegro moderato

4.

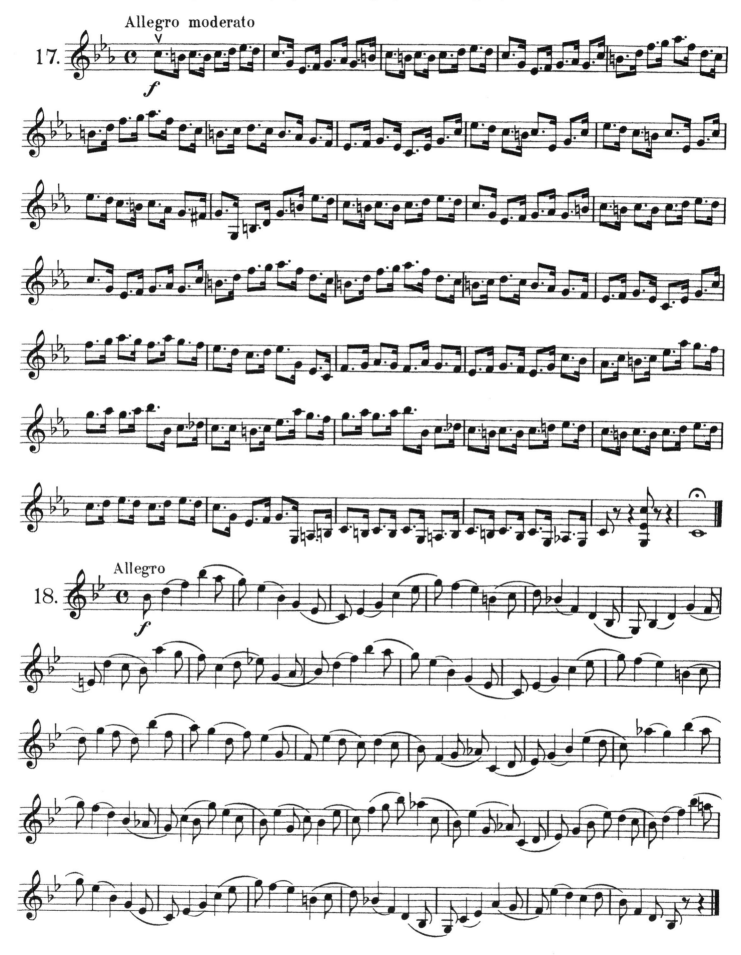

Fifty Easy Melodious Studies
Op. 74, Book II

Franz Wohlfahrt
(1833–1884)

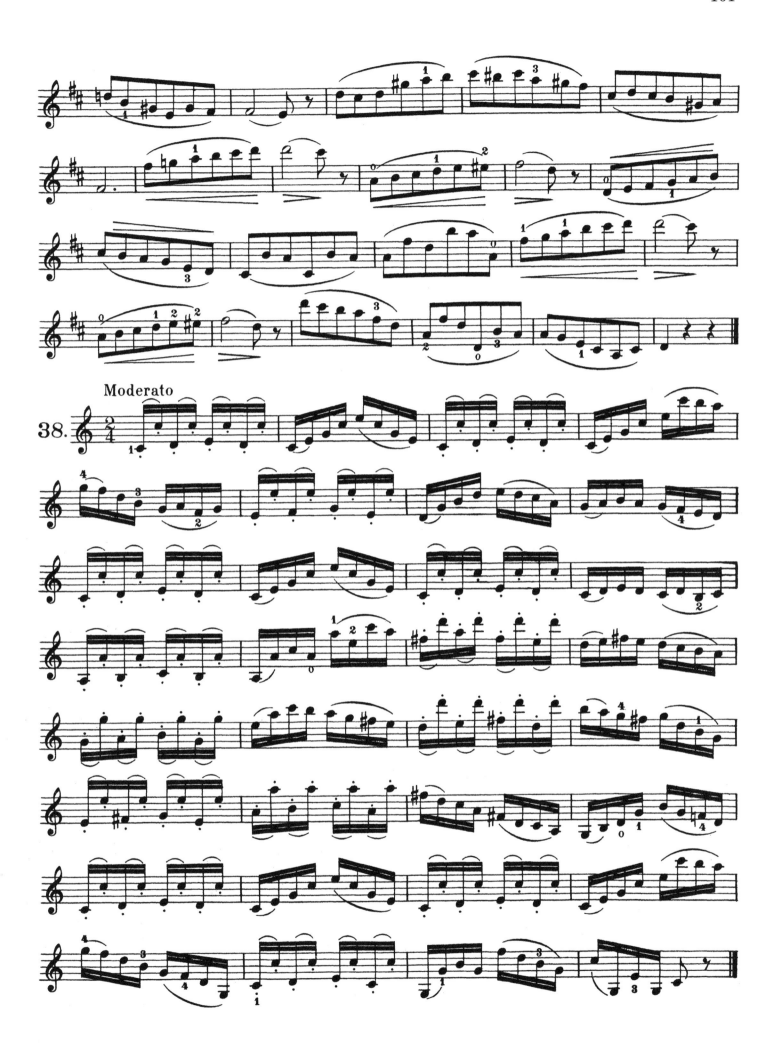

Allegro moderato

47.